Friend of the Court

William Pruitt

Cyberwit.net
HIG 45 Kaushambi Kunj, Kalindipuram
Allahabad - 211011 (U.P.) India
http://www.cyberwit.net
Tel: +(91) 9415091004
E-mail: info@cyberwit.net

Printed at Repro India Limited.

For Steve and Scott,
and for Great Stone,
who built the fire.

Contents

IV.

I.

Owning the Original

How many times, driving west
on Ridge Road, have you seen
the round red midsummer sun
float above the horizon

like something familiar,
like something you put there,
like a print of an original
you could never afford in this life.

If our presumptions slipped away
Even the ants would see

The Light in Provence

Every morning we walk across the Rhone into town or
sometimes ride through the old streets in Marie's e-rickshaw
to the Frank Gehry tower where from the top one can see
a wide stretch of the Camargue plain extending
to the sea   or downstairs to the movie theater for
Phillip Parreno's No More Reality   which does
     magic without tricks   or take a bus
to Saintes-Marie-de-la-Mer and imagine the Mediterranean
as the boundary of everything   and the Viking nightmare
               coming from beyond

Or hop off the bus at Pont de Gau where flamingos—
flamants— appear pale pink in the marsh until
they lift their wings to show bright scarlet   where
the light has a translucent glow on certain mornings

Or when we first get off the train
at the little station in Arles where there are
no cabs or buses or fluent English speakers where
people explain as they can where and what, and
carry our luggage up steep steps unasked   where
Louise Alt Hamoud, standing with her sister and niece,
whose English is not broken but haphazardly assembled ,
and who, as first deputy prosecutor
for the Ministry of Justice
went to Ukraine in 2022
investigating war crimes
for the ICC,

helps us find a taxi.

Las Vegas Blvd.

She stands by the 99¢ Margaritas sign
in front of Bill's Gambling Hall at noon
as pedestrians ignore her placard
that offers free tickets with purchase of
one regular admission   she stands
straight as if suspended by loving gaze
of proud mother and father in Taiwan

She does not need or receive
anything from passers-by
whose blind and soulless random anonymity
cannot displace the one surely heading her way,
who finds she has precisely that
which he had not realized
was missing all his life.

In Paris,

Pedestrians don't look at their cell phones
when they cross the street at intersections,
no matter the walk-signal is green, the not uncommon
red light-running silent cyclists at speed as great
a threat as thundering Harleys and jeeps

Wood pigeon's iridescent sheen burns
into sleep time, pink tugboats push
concrete-hulled barges east, against
the flow of the fussed over Seine

All my dad remembered of Paris is
"where men urinated in public"—
maybe the pissoir was all he could process
after the Battle of Ardennes.
twenty years old, just off the farm.

When Americans came marching down
the Champs-Élysées, what did their faces say?
or was it just their guns people saw?

Today, wood pigeon hoots like an owl in the courtyard.
Olympic bleachers arise by the Arc de Triomphe,
armed guards stand at corners of the eighth arrondissement
their AK-47s as ho-hum as bicyclists
with baguettes sticking out of their packs

In the presidential palace, Macron has been talking to
people all night who swear they can clean up
the Seine in time for the swimming events.

Off the Avenue Montaigne, doorways at storefronts of
Chanel, Dior, Louis Vuitton look out to courtyards
with canopies of hanging golden vines
while cab drivers from Mauritius and Ghana
calculate which streets will be open
when the Games begin.

At the D'Orsay, a roomful of Van Goghs
in an old train station
continues to fill a dark interior
with oracular light
      May, 2024

Interring Anubis

I am doing what you do when you're recovering
from the virus, going through that which
I never use, put on, wear, think about,
when I come across in the floor of my closet
a dark brown miniature ovate case with fitted lid,
a supine figure emerging sarcophagus-like from the top,
the smooth upper half of the lid itself bound
to the weave below by hardened string through
        a circuit of sixteen tiny holes.
Inside,
there's a gold braided cord
attached to a lion's tooth, from Nigeria,
by way of a Canal Street shop in Soho,
a gift from my sister-in-law, "for courage."
        I never wore it,
unwilling to be part of a system of slaughter for profit,
and maybe feeling unworthy to be so close to a king.

But I don't remember how I acquired
        its clandestine partner,
a smaller clear-glass rectangular container
            with hinged lid
showing colorful baroque print lady with parasol,
the miniature chest holding a roughly finished
silvery figure attached to a necklace-length chain
whom I think I know,
but have to check some images to be sure.
Yes,
It's Anubis, jackal-headed Egyptian god of the underworld,

protector of graves— no doubt keeping jackals away —
and inventor of mummification, and I have no idea why
he has stayed among my unnoticed attachments,
halfway across the continent and the century,
next to the guitar I no longer play
and the tooth I've assigned him as buddy.
I have no allegiance to him.

I put the tooth in its woven casket on my desk

Anubis goes where he belongs.
Under the deck. Into the soil.
                        Finally free
of that damned parasol.

Barcelona Gothic District

Narrow passageways   apartment buildings old and dark
offering just enough
room for a car, mostly foot traffic. We see
a man passed out on his knees
face forward on a raised flower bed.
we pass a seated woman mumbling below
a fire escape, I glance to see if she has a cup,
duck into a store as she begins to howl a stream
of curses. No one seems to notice
her hoarse blistering imprecations.
I'm afraid to take a peek in case it's me who roused her.

On to La Rambla and its wide slow walk to the sea
We have champagne at the Erotic Museum
eat delicious sardines at La Plata. On our return,
the passed-out man has awakened to stifled gasping sobs.

The Muse of Ineffable Desire

As he drove to her house, he felt *himself* being driven,
as if something controlled him and the machine
         he controlled,
his hands holding tight to the wheel to keep
desire from extricating him from the car,

He was taking his girl on a date
her eyes warm and green-lit seas across which
they swam the curved and fathomless universe.
He drove in a wonder it had happened to him
her wordless assertion of Yes that revealed the No
he'd thought without thinking was what there was

Her existence proof of that mythical thing
the perpetually dancing goodness machine
at the heart of things, form which he thought
could not be embodied, presence from which
form could not be cleaved

Modern Speeds on Old Roads

I dream I'm lost in thought
while cruising down the parkway,

I hear
an engine roar,
realize I'm doing
one hundred miles an hour
in first gear

My therapist,
whom I didn't tell about this dream,
said Bill, you don't have to
try so hard

Hope
I haven't damaged
the dream transmission

In London

Pedestrians walk briskly on a weekday morning
more or less keeping up with traffic
a bus emits a shattering honk a guy in a derby
not breaking stride turns his head SHADDUP!

On a quiet side street two young men arm in arm
go by a woman waiting for a bus with her little dog
who stares at them intently as they pass
as if she had never come across such a thing

Across from a sprawling Whole Foods in Kensington
people crowd in to a tiny shop stocked with phones
scarves t-shirts UK regalia while the Pakistani owner
connects my phone to internet When a woman looking
for gewgaws for her grandsons hears him speaking
Punjabi or is it Urdu to his assistant, she lets herself fall
off the boardwalk of English onto the connective soil
of Native Tongue He shows her pictures of family
on his phone, their exchange a low flame which gives
the little shop of things a backlit glow

At St. Pancras Station we wait in the train yard to watch
which gate then go underground to stand among
hundreds milling about or at rest where they can find it,
waiting for trains to go under the ocean to Amsterdam,
Belgium or Paris How can all these people
this undifferentiated mass strain out onto
the right track, the right train,
the right car, the right seat,
but they do, without fuss.

Eclipse Unspoiled

sitting & talking in friends' backyard, drinking wine
under overcast sky that keeps darkening
until there comes a completely
different kind of dark

Last Morning in Arles

Her long red hair reflecting
Sun's glimpse into tiny
Alleys of Arles, she sweeps
Her storefront with a pale blue broom

II.

Signs North of the Public Market

Behind glass
white letters on black
in the small fenced front yard
of Faith Deliverance
just opposite Los Primos Deli:
    Hours of Worship

A tabby cat,
discreetly crossing the street,
    headed toward Ruby's Beauty Salon.

On a worn stucco building
above four large windows,
each bordered with white rope lights,
    A frog on a lily pad
    puffing away,
    The Home of Variable Smokes.

From a Distance

A girl in our high school has been attacked, how or by whom she won't say. She is shaky, but when we see her in the hallway she says I'm fine. Later we find her in the girls' restroom, dead.

We see tiny incisions in her skin leading to her heart, which must have caused internal bleeding. She looked okay from a distance, but she was actually cut to pieces. Nothing was holding her together.

The Twenty-Eighth Day

I mistook her for detritus   swept her off
the glass table top   saw tiny legs waving
I flipped her over   she made some more
not-enough-to-go-anywhere moves   I got her
on a cloth napkin and put her up
among the marigolds   The bumblebee
wouldn't let go of her cloth I left her unmoving,
just above the flowers   Clouds passed over
fast and slow   In the morning she was
in the same position   when I nudged her
she rotated   clinging to her cloth like a blanket
she must be in deep meditation, I thought.
In an hour she was gone

Tails Disappearing into the Woods

A rabbit leaps in the high beams of our old car
on a rough winding road with trees crowding in,
I'm a four year-old from the suburbs, amazed
by everything. Saturday morning Lash LaRue.
The cold walls: heat coming from a central stove.
Grandma already making biscuits and gravy,
"Shoog, would you go get some eggs from the henhouse?"
A nameless chicken pecks at me.
They just call the collie "Pup."

How good the slop smelled that Grandpa fed to the pigs,
tomato peels & greens & corn cobs mixed with meal,
cream from the gleaming separator on the screened porch.
    SOOEY SOOEY Grandpa called
and the swine would savor the slop in snorts & grunts,

The cat that caught the stream from the aimed teat,
the cat that bewildered me giving birth in the fruit cellar
the collie that went to summon the cows at
                                        Grandpa's bidding
The horse of my father's boyhood that took him places

Those animals are harder to find now,
tucked away like gigabytes,
consciousness so stunned and diminished
our collie could not bring them back if we had one

Still Waiting

The smell of number two pencil,
     of lined paper from
an open-upward Big Chief notebook.

Why Moses Couldn't Enter the Promised Land

Reading ingredients on a label:
     So this
is process

The Story Is What We Say

1.
Big Bang boring
give me a song
I can handle
Big Bang boring
give me a song
I can sing
how much bang
for the buck

We need a *story*

How about Adam & Eve

How about Remember the Maine?
Remember the Zimmerman telegram?

How about Christ on the cross
How about dying for another's sins

How about sins?
How about this one dying, dying
for that one's freedom

How about letting that nail go right through your hand
How about going the other way, Ayn Rand

A religion of holding on
Or the church of cutting loose

How about just open your hand and look at it

2.

An article in the cultural studies journal *Social Text* asserted in so many words, (in so *many* words) there was no such thing as objective reality. The writer, a mathematical physicist, immediately revealed his piece was a hoax, a parody of social scientists who say the laws of nature are social constructs, of postmodern academics in the humanities who pretend to understand quantum mechanics, and of cultural critics who assert all phenomena can be reduced to sexism or racism or capitalism. The editors had been bamboozled.

Getting past the bloat and babble, the article was actually convincing. How much bang for the buck?

3.
Elizabeth and Maggie Fox
were sisters, heard knocks
This was about the time
William Miller's flock
climbed up Cobbs Hill
to await the end of the world.
They eventually came down
but the Foxes stayed high
getting messages, drinking rum
getting folks to wonder
where those knocks were coming from.
Scientists tested them for truth,
Some were skeptical, others

besotted. Hard to tell the source of those knocks.
Hard to parse the dancer from the dance.

But the year after the Great Blizzard
when Teddy Roosevelt lost his cattle,
had to stop playing gentleman cowboy,
Liz and Maggie confessed it was all
in the joints, all in the big toe.
They had a good run, hurting no one
except a man named Bell, life-long shunned
for the murder of a man whose ghost
was actually Maggie's cracking knuckle.

4.
the color red
the name of a rose
a couple of Benjamins
Universal Standard Time:
It all comes down to gesture,
so much spin
even when the involuntary
nervous system kicks in

the real thing not just the act
but must include what happens after

(pretend/present/represent.
Flaws of representative government:
the bridge gets built or blown up
before the spending bill is passed)

The slaughtered soldier, the Noh drama

Bowman Fish married Leah Fox when she was fourteen,
left her with a daughter and wriggled away to where?

Stanley Fish, another social construct,
published *Social Text,*
complained, "What about trust?"
That physicist pretended there was
a baby in the bathwater skillfully enough
the academic babushkas thought they saw him too,
took him in their arms, he looked a little peakéd
as my grandmother used to say.

Maggie Fox tried to recant her confession, but
her cred with the cognoscenti was shot
she died in poverty, only to learn
those knocks she pretended were strange,

were strange
coming from her own
strange and sacred bones

When Maggie pretended
God was in her big toe.
her greatest sin was making people think
it wasn't so.

It's amazing that baby grew up
surviving on such thin gruel.

Now Maggie Fox beckons
from the gauzy gossamer
of the World Wide Web
(catch her under SPIRITUALISM)

Because she told a story well
Because she gave good bang

The Changeling Simile

When a loved one dies, the mourning never ends.
Instead, it slowly seeps through consciousness
Into deep under-being. Its clammy hand
Comes down with weight on places light had blessed,
Closes its grip on that which would expand,
A stillness now the opposite of rest

But worse for pure life force is foxy change.
What happens when the one who walks beside,
Is similar to, but not the same
Loved companion whose daily sight
Brought solace and release from the soul drain
Of Outside telling Inside things were right.

A small thing gone; a pull-back; light you missed
Made you strangers to each other when you kissed

Nothing Works

Nothing works. Not the confidence thing.
Not self-interest. Not emotion,
or even the ability to cry. Though these
are crucial, if one is to get by when
nothing works. Clarity, understanding,
insight,— all are essential, but not key.

There is no key. Nothing works.
She won't see what you see. She never did.
Love fooled you into thinking that.
How could you be so stupid.
In your eyes, you're blameless. In hers,
you're a little more guilty every day.

The past is not what you thought it was.
The present doesn't go anywhere, like a horse who
knows the body it carries to the grave is not dead.
Let the present stay where it is, where what you have is
nothing but quivering, glowing, expanding, liquid life.

Decorum

In the Civic Center, people summoned for jury duty stood around or sat and waited to be called. Sometimes we read or checked our cell phones, but when we stood, it was clear there were invisible lines we could not cross, postures we could not take, expressions we could not wear, feelings we could not have. We were in a building where law was paramount: enforcement, interpretation, punishment. We had been relieved of our guns and our outdoor minds.

We were shown a movie of how it used to be, in the days when you proved you were innocent by drowning when they tied you to a rock. It's not that way now, they told us, if we accept our responsibility as citizens.

A teen age boy was accused of date rape. It was at a party. The judge was articulate and reasonable. We were called up one by one. Each side took its turn. Have you ever been sexually assaulted? Do you know any policemen? Do you have preconceived ideas?

We missed the ways of counting off the afternoon, the beloved lengthening of shadows, the chores that made history, the trimmings of being alive. Each time someone was called, those of us who were still sitting breathed a little sigh.

Some were excused after they respectfully acknowledged requirements they could not fulfill, or when either side respectfully requested a dismissal based on clear and cited reasons.

Sometimes the judge joined the exchanges. His urbane interjections helped to clarify and relax us in an otherwise cold and forbidding place. We even laughed occasionally. There must have been sixty of us.

When the number of people sitting in the jurors' box reached twenty-five, the judge sent them into a little room with the prosecuting attorney, the defendant's lawyer and the bailiff. It was 3:30. The rest of us twiddled our thumbs. Some of us calculated. *They only need twelve jurors, a couple of extras, the rest of us ought to be able to go home today.*

It would be wrong to say there was any real difference between the people who had gone into the little room and those still waiting to be questioned. Except that some of us outside, delivered into calculating, still hoped to go home, had stopped caring about the girl who was raped and the boy who raped her. Some of us could no more tolerate being in this building than we could stand to be in a cell, putting off being alive indefinitely, a living death, with no crime to atone for.

The door opened at a quarter to five and the bailiff announced, --— We have completed this round of questioning and we have nine jurors for trial

Among those of us waiting to be called, one man uttered a loud groan.

The judge turned his attention from the bailiff to our group. He was not affable. His face was red. — I will have no outbursts! he said angrily. It is a privilege to be a juror! Then his voice became a deep growl. Any more disrespect to the decorum of the court will not go unpunished!

The man had broken decorum, but the judge had shifted tone. He was not smiling. We were afraid of him. He was looking at us, all of us. We had done something very bad.

Yet we were not of the law, we did not belong to the law, and we did not understand why decorum was so important to the law. But we understood that when the bailiff said, —All rise! and we rose, that was only the beginning.

III.

The Supreme Trickster

Joker blowing
Bubbles between smiles
Forget about states' rights
Each *person* has her his
Own bubble of Sovereignty

But we can't see that Person because, Privacy.
A private Self
With Autonomy
Unless you're a woman
Caught in unwanted Pregnancy
Or born with the wrong skin color, trapped in
A pattern of History

Some laws are all about the Self
Its private dreams,

Hold fast to
Framers' Original Thought.
Enshrine the gross mutation
Bind the EPA— watch me now—
So the ability to even have
A private life is swept away
Into the basin of popping bubbles,
Cauldron of climate nightmare,

Just pulling your leg, says Joker

The Mayflower Correction

Our immigrant classmate told his people's story,
how his ancestors had been reduced
by hunger and climate change to
a few score on a sandy strip of land.

Of how a hurricane would have finished them off
if not for a great fish come from the depths
carrying them through black shark water
to soft breeze green place with black soil.

Our teacher smiled, said *interesting*
then turned to the core curriculum of History,
and told us about the Pilgrims searching
here and there for their rights

because it had to be
because how else
could things have turned out
the way they did

How they sat at table with Noble Indian
as if Plymouth were Virginia,
as if the ten weeks of hell they sailed through
at peak of storm season because the ship left late

were not even a footnote,
would not appear on a test

In the Cloisters

(five men and four women seated around a table).

First Justice. —What say you, Justice Two?

Second Justice. —What do the tea leaves say?

First Justice —What say thee, Justice Three?

Justice three— Read the entrails. *That's* where the truth is.

 First Justice. —Anything more, Justice Four?

Justice Four. —What did the Founders intend?
They thought in a certain way.
I have studied a lifetime to see
what they wanted to say.
Only the strictest constructionist
can tease out the grand design.

First Justice. —Still alive, Justice Five?

Justice Five: —Words, words, words.

First Justice. — Justice Six, any more tricks?

Justice Six — No matter what, we have to ensure the supply of kids.

First Justice. —Why would that be?

Justice Six: To keep the Dragon gorged of course.

First Justice. —Justice Seven through Nine, we're running out of time.

Justice Seven through Nine. (heads in hands) —Word.

First Justice— Your thoughts?

Justice Seven through Nine. —You want thoughts or lament?
A path to what works or a screed on the Founders' intent?
Don't bother us now, we're busy tearing up and tearing up
Amendments and articles to sew shreds into shrouds
to cover our shame to be in this frame
of women's screams and our
beloved planet's flames.

Amicus Curiae in Igne

Amicus curiae: an individual or organization who is not a party to
a legal case, but who is permitted to assist a court by offering
information, expertise, or insight that has a bearing on the issues
in the case.

First Candle
None of the news sources looked too closely.
Did he use fire starter? What was he wearing?
How did he carry himself? There was a photo of him
sitting with his head on fire. Were there sounds?
Several feeds said there was no letter or manifesto,
Some linked it to a shooter of random pedestrians
across town who then killed himself.
calling it "a day of chaos" for the city,
the hotline number at end of story
"if you or someone you know is in crisis..."

How about
all of us?

There will be a follow up piece
on what made Wynn Bruce different,
but not on what made him like the rest of us,
how the world he lived in is ours.
A few witnesses will be questioned.
Some may admit to shielding their eyes
as we do when a pattern takes form and we blink
not necessarily from brightness but from

the dark, where shapes
begin to achieve definition

The *someday* Sununu said meant *we don't know,*
single-handedly crushing consensus in Reagan's America
now giving way to the Delphic *soon.*
Wynn Bruce combusted into metaphor.

Second Candle
If war is metaphor where someone actually has to die
what Wynn Bruce did was the ultimate act of war
the emphatic No that Melville imagined for Bartleby.

No to who we are, (an aggregate of selves
                    blind to our ensemble).

No to the ignorance we praise and the fear we enshrine
No to the suicidal Lie that passes as a means to an end
No to the life which permits this miscarriage

No to every man for himself
No to man
No to self
that self finally saying the final No
                    "I would prefer not to."

Third Candle
Three of you,

sweet young girl,
drop-dread gorgeous mother,
battle-scarred crone,

your root-like links go down into Earth
Whose mycelial neurons let trees connect

Who saw the stars form, who sees geese cross
the Great Lakes every spring & every fall,
hears them honk as they land with a splash
Triple Goddess, you saw Wynn Bruce die,
in the ocean of your existence felt one tear fall

It's hard to imagine,
hard to conceive the size of compassion
hard to think this act would come from such passion

Fourth Candle
Praise for Wynn Bruce!
Who chanted his searing song
on Earth Day in front of the Court
whose majority say Earth has no defense
against men who would choke her to death
as if Justices said to Derek Chauvin
You don't have to lift your knee
by a six to three majority.

Fifth Candle
Our disease is who and what we think we are,
it's the one that's had no research, so no cure.
Yesterday our fathers came home exhausted from war.
We grew up thinking we were living in peace
except for the atrocity at Wounded Knee
we may or may not have learned of in school
and the Moro Crater massacre
we certainly did not learn of in school
and Little Rock, where we tried to stop
some of our own children from coming to school
and Selma, where we tried to keep some
of our own people from voting out fools

and My Lai where we couldn't shield our eyes
and the glacier and the coral reef
we thought weren't in the image of God
and the frogs and songbirds also deemed expendable,
just call it Nature, kill so self can live to kill again,
the same self
Wynn Bruce showed
could be torched

Journalists and historians told the story
but the message didn't come through all the way
the news didn't quite get delivered
the ink that linked the dots didn't stay

till we finally got it!
We never were at peace
there was just a break in the carnage
the Fascist repaired to his den
you think the monster's dead
but look he lifts his head again.
Your zombie neighbor's too hungry
to think of the planet. He's been living too long
on massive pictures of food on the sides of trucks

Sixth Candle
An under-reported act that was
the opposite of "random." Was it suicide?
Is it suicide to write a poem? Auden said poetry
makes nothing happen but is it supposed to?
Isn't to make an impression to take something away?
Displace the reader's sense of time with the poem's own?

Seventh Candle
Los was the poet and smith of William Blake's epic,
the divine aspect of the imagination, the one

who works to bring the sacred into human action.
Los was a poet who forged, carved into rock,
engraved with burning stylus. He worked to make
creation prevail over his brothers' impulse to destroy.
Los used abrasives & polishers, gouges, chisels & gravers,
sharp-tipped pens to make what he saw come alive

Eighth Candle
The Peacemaker climbed the roof
of the cannibal's house and
with perfect timing, looked
down through the smoke hole
just as the wild man looked into the pot
to see if dinner was ready, and thought
he saw his own face reflected & said

"I did not know I was that kind of man,"
lost his taste for human flesh.

This is not my story, but one
the Haudenosaunee tell,

Could it be our story?

May it become our story.

 Wynn Bruce immolated himself in front of the Supreme Court on
Earth Day 2022

Moro Crater Massacre- 1906. American soldiers put down a
rebellion of Filipinos by firing into the dormant volcanic crater
they were hiding in and killing all but a handful of many hundreds
of women, men and children "insurgents."

Pay Now or Pay Later

Pay now or pay later God said when we plundered the land
and we said

Already paid,
our pioneers butchered,
our gravid women scalped,
fetuses ripped from womb,
nailed to fence like the devil's greeting
worse than animals, the cunning savage

God wasn't fooled. *We* were the cunning ones, our religion
had taught us there was a heaven and it was tomorrow.
Today the best we could do in this fallen wound of a world
      was to be on top
so we learned in our cradles how to say *later*

At night on the middle passage: moaning cargo
keening from the hold assailed the captain's ears

Some of them will get through he said
and God said *pay now or pay later*

Captain said *They're not like us.*
They were already slaves when we found them.
They'll be better off here among Christians..

Yet as the call for bids went out
on the sunlit auction block
We knew in our smudged moral accounting

a cost not entered in the books
We trimmed the loose ends of our hearts & said
later

People came here to be free,
so even the Free Staters had to agree
    there's got to be cotton for planting
so it can be sold to the north who can then produce guns
    to build a safe place when people flee homelands.
And if we look for a silver lining we'll find one
as long we're warm and well fed when we look
    A slave is a slave we said,
we'll pay later
        and some said
        war & amendments took
   the poison plant away

        but the spilled blood only watered
   the roots left intact,
        roots that could neither read
nor understand amendments.

We fought wars against those
the exiles were fleeing
but as people kept bolting the tyrant's grasp

we threw up our hands and started shooting at *them*
pretending it was always the tyrants our friends
and God said...
       • • • •

Now we have switched to a new pretense
We say we use critical thinking
we're being selective with science

    But the haves who back murder forgot
    in their drowse they no longer
    believe in that *later* they promise is coming
Why not take the profit now they say

How long before we stop pretending
that anyone is listening but our own hearts,
where God lives, who has sensitive ears, can't hear
over the noise, the whale-piercing roar of these frenzied days
How long before God says, *I can't hear you. Did you say now?*

Uvalde

Instead of having a moment of silence
to remember them after,

Let us have a moment of blindness
to remember ourselves

who could not remember them *before*.

Minotaur

Perhaps this is what you were taught: *Queen Pasiphae slept with a bull sent by Poseidon, and gave birth to the Minotaur, a creature half man, half bull. King Minos was mortified, but did not want to kill a creature of divine origin, so he hid the monster in a* **Labyrinth** *which was constructed by Daedalus at the Minoan Palace of Knossos. He fed the sacred creature young people until Theseus arrived and slew it.*

This is a version our schools have given us, so all can say we've been taught the Greek myths.

Let me tell you.

It has been closed in for so long it doesn't know about anything except hunger, and the terror it sees in the eyes of its victims.

It doesn't know about circumstance.

King Minos had prayed for a sacred bull from Poseidon which he promised to offer as sacrifice, but when that time came, he decided the bull was too sacred to kill. Another would do in its place.

So this king forgot that sacrifice was a metaphor for a clean break from attachment, coin of the realm to show the human is free and godlike. Instead he put himself above Poseidon, which made the king's will— and his unity with the divine— subservient to his own attachment. This invited the greater powers to shred it.

The Queen was intrigued, aroused by this transcendent beast. She fucked the Sacred Bull. She bore a monster.

The Minotaur knows nothing of this— how could it? It lives through its victims, who experience it as inhuman— not seeing its human mother, a queen, a woman whose breasts have suckled babies,— its victims know only this thing which waits to devour them, just as we readers of adulterated versions see only the wanton wife, the humbled king, the chaos and carnage till the coming of Theseus, the great warrior. We miss the lesson: how the way to live is by the model that our parents betrayed, if we keep our promises, respect the great forces, and understand our fate is not entirely in our hands. Because no matter how much knowledge we accrue, how much wisdom we may haply grab, we are all conceived in circumstance.

IV.

After Rain

After rain, the air is cool.
The big lake has high clouds.
Summer didn't wear us out this year.
This morning my daughter returns
to school. Her absence is choired
in mist that rises from the mountain pond.
Crow calls to a white ruckus in the east.
The desire for ecstasy has been replaced
by the desire to see.

Check Out

What is that zone
where what you see
looking into someone's eyes,
meets what they see?

She's cashiering,
knows her job well enough
to sometimes let her dark eyes
not look at any thing

What is beauty? Skin or structure,
or what shines through? Lips & eyes?
or the smile or sadness present there?
Does she see what she is anywhere?

There's a field around her,
a weightless liquid aura,
radiant cloud from within which she
surveys the domain
of grace as far
as eye can see.

Bagging cranberries
and beer,
she's laughing with two Puerto Rican women
checking out in front of me.
Why is she laughing, I need to know,
moving up as they go. As if knowing my mind,
she volunteers, "They thought I was Hispanic."

What does it mean, to be in her presence.
I hand her a head of cauliflower.
Unasked, she explains she is Polish.
She doesn't know she's different.
it makes no difference that she sees me.
She can't see what I see, and I
will never know what hit me
I'm part of a strangeness just for a moment
But the song she brings just gives me the blues.

Letting Go of Now

I am sitting in a graduate class which M, who is my age, is teaching. There are fifteen to twenty students, all in their mid-twenties or late teens. M is extemporizing as he likes to do. A memory comes to him. He says, "I remember this girl, she was so nice. Beautiful eyes, slim waist." At this, everyone says, spontaneously, "Shut up! Be quiet!"

M stops, stunned. I had tried to warn him with my eyes, but he hadn't seen me. At first I think he is going to calmly reflect in his usual style of detachment, until I see he is shaken. One tear drops from his eye, then more, although he is silent. I think of something to say, and stand to address the class, but most people have left the room. They have treated M's silence as the equivalent of a break.

But when I go out of the room, people are quiet, pensive. One strong and volatile young woman embraces me. It's not simply a hug. We are locked. Another does the same to M when he comes out. Everyone is quietly, physically communing.

I wait to speak till we go back in:

"Everyone here has an idea of what she or he thinks is the real thing. But some day you will understand that this is it. And you will respond to the spontaneous sharing of a memory from within the natural confines of yourself, instead of from this socially constricting platform you're standing on. And you will understand how memory can be like petting a cat."

"But what about the treachery of memory?" says the woman who hugged me.

"It's not about that."

Peace

Behind my back, the hidden full moon
In front of me, tiny waves keep going peacefully to the beach.
The lake, an almost color-drained rose, reflecting a sky
the sun had gone out of, a rose becoming coral.

But where are so many small waves going?
Leftward, animate, identical multiple ripplings,
waves moving shoreward till the water's gone
But how can waves run out of water?

Left to right, my head is tilted,
but the lake doesn't spill. Water darkens,
in the foreground of the shadows,
something moves, a shadow wave.

Dark Energy

You like to think there's a neutral moment
where what's there is there and you wonder
what it is that makes you uneasy

until you understand
there is an invisible weight
pressing down like gravity, but malign,

bent on suppressing every impulse
towards joy and interdependence, and you wonder
at its utter invisibility and how you have managed

to escape until you see you haven't,
if it suppresses those whom you feel things through,
it suppresses you

Why Noah's Ark No Longer Floats

The old Evangelist stepped out one bright
summer morning, and thought, *Why couldn't
God make it rain forty days and forty nights?
Why can't the secular mind accept the possibility?
Because Science is a failure of imagination!*

Yet Darwin imagined deeply how the land subsided
on which the coral reefs were formed.
He observed effect and wondered cause,
he and his mistress Nature working backward
through unfolding intimate time.

They both cried in fear her father was dead.
They kept on together, risking opprobrium,
keeping their discoveries semi-secret,
until they found she was not an orphan,
but immaculately conceived,

But Darwin's staff didn't wriggle like a snake,
and true believers said that can't be right.
So it was those who denied the science who failed.
(The preacher had confused *imagine* with *believe*.)

As everyone's time line became contingent on creed
Darwin's mistress became belittled, debased,
along with the question of where *we* began.

.

I could have told the preacher if he had asked.
We've always been here,
telling stories.

But today the tales that include instructions
for constructing an ark to deliver the faithful
from the fate of the Earth and from hapless humans

are code for building a sinking tomb,
from portions of eternity each one's birthright
which too long unused become unstable
those blocks of light now bars of plutonium
a pyramid scheme with a half-life smile
from the Cheshire cat
who vanishes at
"All Aboard!"

Skaneateles

"Had we but world enough and time"
Andrew Marvell

Honey bee in the dame's rocket
catbird on the Northern White Cedar
my wife gets a massage across the road
while I sit before a meadow at sunrise

It's a springing path the limbs of the Norway
spruce provide for gray squirrel, whose
destination may change but is never in doubt

Song sparrow lands on a vine coming off
the spruce to get a look at me. Thank you
for noticing, bird with beautiful song, enhanced
by sundial lupine bumblebee thunder

At my back, time's turbo charged chariots I hear
paint the minute particulars with
A wide and blustering swath

A white strand of nothing hangs from nothingness.

Impossible you say? No more than the guy
obliterating a world he doesn't have enough of.

Catching Breath

Divide the world, you miss it
Skip a beat, it's gone
Try to hold it together,
It slips away

The one displaced or lost or unattached
Is the one who hears my poem.

Only when her breath catches
As I read aloud the passage that
Caught mine when I wrote it,
Is the world real.

We shouldn't charge too much for poems
The ones who are most moved by them
May be the ones who've given up
Trying to hold it all together

The Fury of Being

those of us who
the greatest threat do see—
not in the choosing mode of this or that—
are if you've noticed
in the minority

so, what is most essential is to be.
it may enable others to see
what we see

now, some may have carefully thought-out
opinions but
fail to truly see
which can keep them
out of sync with
what they think
is reality.

not to oppose stridently.
today, the greater opposition is to be
it's not like times of old
when it was about which party

today is not so much to be free
but having room to be
it's flapping our wings
and letting ourselves expand
while we can
and seeing if we can let others see what we see

maybe somehow see past
what they are told they see

don't let them catch you seeing
their agitated selves in your eyes
which keeps them from seeing what you see
don't let them catch you at all

As money makes money,
clouds make clouds
don't let those blinded
by clouds in their eyes
confuse their clouds with yours
give clouds a pass
to leave the eyes of the blinded,
let them see past
what they are told they see

don't let us all be blinkered
into a new Dark Age

let us continue
to discover what
is,

and what it is
to be

Aubade

moist wind in leaves at dawn
loved ones still sleeping, new
moon long gone, light comes
to sunflowers   corn
morning glory runner beans
zucchini chicory
green tomato Rose of Sharon

look at the sunflower, see
how its center is composed of
tiny separate flowers, how their
arrangement on the disc resembles pinwheels?
growing along the fence their melancholy
is most evident at dusk and on cloudy mornings

I would like
to slip into bed
and wake those loved ones
like the sunflowers
woke me this morning
looking at me
till I dreamt of them
& awoke

Deep Bright

She was watering the mums,
purple, orange, cinnamon, scarlet,
her dense black-brown braids
a deeper bright than the flowers,
bright like her brown skin, reflecting
the big bright pumpkins she stood behind,
all of us bright on the parking lot
 in the late October sunrise

Desert Signage

People in cars
are stopping at
an unsigned
monument in the desert,
a small gray slab in the sand.

Does it represent something,
or is it a magnetic force?
No one speaks, or is it
just that we can't hear them?

There's no one in charge
They seem to know
why they are there, getting out
then back in to their cars.
They come and go like birds

acknowledgments

These poems, or versions of them, appeared n the following publications:

"Amicus Curiae in Ignis"
"Pay Now or Pay Later"
        Adelaide Literary Journal

"Interring Anubis"
"Modern Speech on Old Roads"
"The Muse of Ineffable Desire,"
"Owning the Original"
"Signs North of the Public Market"
        BlazeVOX

"Check Out"
 "Peace"
        Bold Cities and Golden Plains (chapbook)

"Desert Signal"
        Le Mot Juste 23

"After Rain"
        Longhouse

"Decorum"
        Visitant

"Dark Energy" (as "Dark Matter")

Walking Home from the Eastman House (book)

"Aubade"
White Pine Journal (untitled)

William Pruitt has published eight books of fiction and poetry and has told original stories in such places as the Rochester Museum and Science Center and the National Women's Hall of Fame. He has written over a thousand critiques as first reader of submissions to Narrative Magazine. He taught English for 26 years to non-native speakers while working for BOCES, the University of Rochester and the New York State Migrant Education Department. He and his wife Pam have a daughter and son, and two grandchildren.